# STREET SMART
# PERSUASION

## How To Sell More Using The Power OF Your Written And Spoken Words

**Foreword By Ben Gay, III**

**Michael "Mike D." Dolpies**

© Copyright 2012 Michael J. Dolpies

Printed in the U.S.A

Published By: Ocean View Publishing, LLC

Street Smart Persuasion, How to Sell More Using the Power of Your Written and Spoken Words
Dolpies, Michael J. 1979-

Business, Sales, Marketing
ISBN-10: 0979910412
ISBN-13: 978-0979910418

**Disclaimer:**
The purpose of this book is to educate and entertain. The author and publisher does not guarantee that anyone following the techniques, suggestions, ideas and strategies will become successful. The author and publisher shall have neither, liability nor responsibility to anyone with respect to any loss or damage caused, or alleged to be caused, directly or indirectly by the information contained in this book.

# PASSING THE TORCH

In 1979, I discovered a most unusual book, *The Closers*. It was in very rough form and only 500 copies had been printed. I bought them all, acquired the publishing rights, edited it, promoted it, and turned it and its audio program into the all-time favorites of salespeople all over the world. *The Closers* has been good to me . . . and vice versa!

I mention this because the same year *The Closers* was born also marked the birth of a bright future protégé of mine, Mike Dolpies. I am proud to say that Mike was - and still is - one of my "students!" But Mike is also now a fine master teacher in his own right, and more importantly for you, a practitioner of the art of persuasion, influence and closing sales. His research is sound and you can easily profit from his real world experience.

In this sharp, concise book you now hold in your hands, Mike guides you through the art of ethical persuasion in a simple straightforward manner that will turn amateurs into pros and pros into masters.

For those of us who have been helping companies and individuals close more sales through our books, seminars and audio/video programs for many years, we are relieved to know that a man such as Mike Dolpies is someone to whom we can pass the torch.

All the best!


# BFG3

Ben Gay III
*THE CLOSERS*
WWW.BFG3.COM

# A Quick Note From The Author

What is "Street Smart?"

When I use the term "Street Smart" I use it interchangeably with "Real World" and "Real Business." I grew up in inner city Philadelphia. I received two educations: one in the classroom and one on the street. In business (and life) we all need two educations, the academic and the real world. The street lessons are the ones that you learn with greater pain. But the street lessons make you wise and are easily applied to your next situation.

On the "streets" of the business world (or life) there is no one skill that will serve you better than the skill of ethical persuasion. The ability to ethically persuade using your spoken and written words will carry you far when you combine them with your other marketable skills.

Street Smart Persuasion is simply, real life persuasion. Persuasive principles that will work for you.

## And Here's The Truth...

You only need a few sound principles to do well in the world of persuasion, selling and influence. Chances are that your competitor does not read books like this in his free time. Chances are he watches TV.

John Francis Tighe was a wildly successful copywriter (written word persuasion). Many, many years ago he said...

"In the land of the blind, the one-eyed man is king."

(Or, one-eyed woman is queen depending on your degree of political correctness.)

Many have heard that - but few actually get it. The fact of the matter is there are certain skill sets, certain techniques and certain methods that many are "blind" to. They can't see them and most people are totally unaware that they exist.

**Like the "Kiss of the Dragon," it's powerful, but doesn't take long to learn!**

You might be thinking, "What is this guy talking about, Kiss of the Dragon?" As a martial arts guy and Tae-Kwon-Do black belt I have seen my share of martial arts flicks. "The Kiss of the Dragon" was a movie that Jet Li did in the year 2000. At the end of the movie, he kills the lead bad guy using "The Kiss of the Dragon." That's when he places a small needle in a certain area of the bad guy's neck causing blood to rush to his brain leading to a slow, painful death.

Scary picture I know, but let me ask you this. If that technique was actually possible, how long would it take Jet Li's character to actually teach it to you? Seems to me that it would just be a matter of knowing where to put the needle right?

So you'd go in to see Jet Li, he take a few minutes and show you how it works and then you'd be all set with "The Kiss of the Dragon" and be able to save the world too.

As you'll discover, business, marketing, selling and influence are really a matter of knowing where to put the needle, so let's get started!

Have Fun!

"Mike D."

This book is dedicated to my wife Jamie and our two little "sweeties," Julia and Marissa, true masters of the art of persuasion.

# Table of Contents

# Author's Preface - The More Doors Open Phenomenon

Think you have to earn all A's at a top business school to be successful? Think again. Many entrepreneurs, salespeople and individuals that have earned the highest accomplishments have been proverbial C-students. I graduated in the percentage of the class that made the bottom half possible! Every now and then, when I have to put down my "formal" education level for some questionnaire I always write; Close to Ivy League Grad. My wife graduated from Cornell, so that makes me "Close to an Ivy League Grad!"

These secrets can help you shortcut your path to success. Unexpected doors will open for you. It's what I call *the more doors open phenomenon.* It means that when you make a decision to do one thing, whether it's the wrong or right decision, more doors open as a result of the decision. The doors that open are ones that you never thought would open, but have as a result of your decision.

Explaining the "more doors open phenomenon" in general terms may seem a bit confusing. Let's look at an example to demonstrate how it works. Let's say that you are interested in mastering a new skill. You want to learn this valuable skill. You search the marketplace and find a course that makes acquiring this skill simple. Your initial goal was to learn a new skill, which you do, but more doors were opened that you didn't expect. For example, in the course a book is recommended. You take the advice and buy the recommended book. Little did you know at the time, but by buying the book you have just opened more doors on the way to your success.

You finish reading the book a week after it arrives. The book is an excellent resource and recommends a second book. You purchase the second book and devour it. The second book opens another door because it has a phone number in it. You call the number on a Saturday night expecting to receive voicemail. Yet, another door opens because a person actually answers the call.

The person on the phone is the author of the book you just read. By speaking to him directly another door has been opened. You form a friendship and work together on business projects. You help each other and in the process you both benefit and others do too. Ben Gay, III wrote the foreword for this book. I just told you the story of how I met him.

Now rewind back to the first door you opened. Which door was it? The door you walked through when you decided to invest in yourself. That decision ballooned into many more opportunities. This is a prime example of the "more doors open phenomenon."

Look at your business. What decisions have you made in the past and how did they affect your future? Did a bad decision lead to a devastating mistake or did it save you from an even worse fate? Did a good decision lead to a string of events to speed up your success? Some people say that everything happens for a reason, the "more doors phenomenon" plays into this thinking. You're reading these words for a reason!

Take time to analyze your business and track how doors have opened for you. Also realize that by making decisions you will enjoy successes and events that you didn't think were possible or didn't even know existed.

I guess you've either made the decision to invest in this book and further your knowledge of the art of influence and persuasion or you are still "thinking about it." Just imagine the possibilities.

What doors are about to be opened for you? I am excited for you! Feel free to contact me and let me know about your success. Go www.askmiked.com and register for my e-newsletter.

# Introduction

Let's face it; everything comes down to the written and spoken word! The internet, social media, one on one interpersonal communication – everything! I don't care what business you're in, what you sell or what you do. How you communicate verbally and in writing will determine your success.

One thing I discovered when I opened my first business at the age of eighteen, just six months out of high school, was simple: If I wanted to survive then thrive I had to persuade people with my words.

In today's business environment, you need to know what to say and what to write! While communication has increased it is now extremely tough to get face to face with someone. You'll frequently find yourself typing emails and sales letters to clients and perspective clients. You'll be checking out LinkedIn Profiles and communicating via social media. If you don't know what to say during these opportunities you're dead before you get started!

I consult with companies and sales people in a variety of different industries. And one thing that is certain is the overwhelming evidence that those of us who are more persuasive lead happier, wealthier, and more fulfilled lives. We get to do what we want to do and we choose what we want others to do, then, we persuade them to do it.

## Why, Street Smart?

As a city kid, "the street" is where my roots are. I believe that you can learn a whole lot there. I have nothing against academics. Academics are essential. But I do know from firsthand experience and the input of many friends and colleagues that "the street" is where you get your education. On the "street" quick thinking persuasive skills will determine your success.

There are a whole lot of master persuaders that use these skills to deceive others. This book is not written for them! It's written for you. The person who has good intentions, a quality product or service, and good things to offer your fellow human beings.

When you quickly master the art of persuasion, you'll not only have the tools to use for yourself, but you'll know how to defend yourself against those whose intentions are not good or beneficial to you. Armed with this knowledge you'll never be a sucker again!

Even more fun and rewarding for you is the fact that you'll now be able to get *yes's* where before all you had was *no's*.

Be sure to mark this book up (unless you borrowed it from a friend, in that case get one of your own!). Refer to it often and share it with your friends and colleagues.

# The Ultimate Success Formula

Use the right words

Say them the right way

At the right time

To the right people

Remember...

What comes out of your mouth and goes on your businesses promotional materials = Your Success

"Don't be a slave to precedent. It is an enemy of progress. Know the techniques of Persuasion, but keep your mind open. Study people at the top and then ask yourself, "Why can't I do what they have done?" Resolve TO BE MORE THAN JUST AVERAGE!

YOU WILL SUCCEED WHEN YOU:

- Thoroughly believe in what you are selling.
- Are tactful and know how to approach people.
- Get to the point quickly.

- Focus.
- Are reliable
- Keep your promises.
- Approach with the conviction that you will get a yes.
- Work Hard
- Always look out for the person at the other end of the bargain.
- Don't oversell or undersell your case.

# Street Smart Secret # 1 - You Must Persuade Yourself First

Think of the times when you were persuaded to make a purchase or take some sort of action by another person. Now, think of some times when you decided against a purchase or action. The one variable beyond cost or timing was inevitably the person that was attempting to persuade you. Then, when you dig deeper, the next wild card was their belief in themselves.

Human beings can't help it – our attitudes and emotions are contagious. It's like the movie "Fallen" with Denzel Washington that was made in my hometown of Philadelphia. The evil spirit would jump from body to body at will. That's what our emotions and attitudes do – they jump from person to person.

In order for anyone to be moved by your spoken or written words, everything you say and write must be totally congruent and believable. Pay attention to these five areas:

### 1) You've got to believe in you

You have to convince yourself that you deserve everything in life you desire. Your self-image and picture you have of yourself needs to be that of a winner. When you look in the mirror you have to be happy: physically, emotionally, mentally and spiritually. Here's how...

Take care of yourself! Exercise daily; eat a reasonably healthy diet (Not too many Philly Cheesesteaks). Constantly increase your flow of positive useful and practical knowledge. Invest in yourself because there is no other investment that will pay off more.

## 2) Have good talks with yourself

The most important person that can ever say anything to you is yourself. Your dialog is being recorded by your subconscious mind. That powerful force will believe everything you tell it. It'll cause you to act in a way consistent with the picture you are painting of yourself. If you wouldn't say to someone else – don't say it to yourself.

Here try this... say to yourself: "I'm no good, I suck, I'm a loser." How to you feel? Pretty crappy I'll bet! Now try this... say to yourself: "I am the man, Oh – I'm good, I'm powerful, I'm persuasive, I get what I want!" Feels good right? Now, it's not all you have to do but it does beat the other option.

I have the habit of talking to myself and communicating my goals to myself while I am engaged in ordinary tasks. Next time you are washing dishes or straightening up after the kids, don't grumble and complain, recite your goals. It goes like this…

"I earn $500,000.00 per year," "I am a leader in my field," "My house is paid off free and clear!" You get the idea. Try it, it's fun! How does this relate to persuasion? Because as you drive these affirmations deep into your subconscious you begin to act in a way congruent with the affirmations which will help you sell more, do more, and be more so that you can live up to your subconscious beliefs.

### 3) Don't listen to the folks that want to drag you down! They are, as I like to say, B-R-U-T-A-L!

Unfortunately, some of them have the same last name as you or they have your spouse's maiden name! Let it go in one ear and out of the other. My mother-in-law lived with us for a short while because my wife's father past away young and left her in a tough financial position. She was a big help with the kids because Jamie and I both work.  She and I just didn't mix well, though!

The fact that I don't swing a hammer or carry a tape measure doesn't sit right with her. Believe it or not, she does not understand what I do and used to frequently question it. Her favorite one was; "All you do is talk on the phone all day!" That's right, I do! I'm always on the phone with clients who are paying me good money for my help with their marketing and selling systems. To this day she still feels as though I'm not good enough for Jamie! I just let her know that a good sales presentation goes a long way!

The point is this: I don't have to explain what I do to her! But, of more importance, I did not let her negative comments drag me down. If I had let her influence me I'd have been out looking for work as a laborer instead of writing and promoting this book. If you wonder what planet some people are from you are not alone – I'm with you!

### 4) You must believe in your message/product/service.

Unless you don't care about the relationships you have with others; your own reputation, or don't mind not sleeping well at night you really have to know in your heart that you have a good quality message, product, or service. Not believing in what you're offering will make you less effective when trying to convince others. I know some can get by deceiving others, but eventually it catches up with them and they fall flat on their faces.

Take it from me; I've got a degree from the school of hard knocks. I once jumped in to an expensive business venture only to lose a ton of money. Main reason: At the core, I did not believe in what I was doing. I plead youthful ignorance and being naive to that one. It was a lesson that I paid close to $200,000.00 and almost two years of my life for.

## 5) You have to be passionate about what you're doing

Chris Gardner is the real life story behind the movie, *The Pursuit of Happiness* that stared Will Smith. If you saw the movie you know that he was a struggling, homeless, single parent. But he used his passion for math and people to become widely successful in the investment banking business.

The reason why most folks lead (what they would consider to be) mediocre lives is because they are not really doing what they want or are passionate about. To be persuasive you must be passionate! So either get excited about what you're doing or get doing what makes you excited.

If I ever find myself in a situation where I am clearly in over my head or feeling nervous I let my passion take over! I keep reassuring myself that my mission is important and that what I am offering is going to enhance the other person's life when they say 'yes' to me. We both win! Of course don't be silly and think passion alone will do it.

When I work with new sales people or business owners the first thing I do is help them reinforce their belief in what they are selling. I was coaching someone new to the game of persuasion that was off to a rough start. After a few failed presentations we found the mental block that was holding her back. Her true passion was not coming through because she kept telling herself that she could not afford what she was selling. I made her realize that she was not the buyer she was the seller.

I related my own experience of a time when I invested $50,000 of my savings to open a new business. When I put out the money to open my business I would not have been able to purchase my own service! I simply did not have the cash. I missed some sales because of this mental block. But then I remembered that I was not the buyer I was the seller. Do you think most of the guys selling jets to big time executives can purchase their own? I'd wager that most of them can't, no big deal, they are the sellers not the buyers.

So get passionate about what you're doing and get rid of the mental and emotional baggage.

# Street Smart Secret # 2- Use The Right Words and Keep it Simple

Use the right words that make people say yes!

I originally learned this concept from Master Sales Trainer and Best Selling Author, Tom Hopkins. He said that there are *go* words and *scare* words. There are words that influence and words that make people resistant to being influenced.

I put this concept into practice in my own business and watched my persuasive power increase many times over.

Watch this....
If I said this to you wouldn't it scare the crap out of you?

"We will schedule an appointment and talk about the prices, then you can buy one of our products. Once we complete the order form I'll do the contract. After that I'll send it to the billing company for collection."

Yikes!

Believe it or not many people in business communicate this way with potential customers without even knowing it. This causes their potential customers to grab their pocket books and run for the hills!

## Remove from your vocabulary the following underlined words

Replace price with *investment, tuition* or *amount.*

Replace contract with *agreement, understanding, paperwork, application* or *form.*

Replace order form with *action form, enrollment form* or *acceptance form.*

Replace billing/collection company with *outside service.*

Replace appointment with *arrange a visit, make a special time* or *set a convenient time to answer all of your questions.*

Replace Buy Now with *Why don't we get the ball rolling?*

Do you see how using these words will help you melt away someone's resistance? They are friendlier and show the other person what is in it for them.

David Garfinkel gave me a few more great words that I always put into my verbal and written communication. The words are *quickly, easily, naturally, you're invited, announcing and amazing.* Out of context these words may just seem like normal words, no big deal, but look at this example he once pointed out to me.

Suppose you go to your local auto dealer and, very abruptly, the salesperson says, "Take the car for a test drive!" A little harsh, right? Now, what if he says, "*You're invited* to take this car for a test drive." See the difference. One more:

If I said to you, "I've got this new book I want to tell you about!" No big deal! If I say, "I've got this *amazing* new book I want to tell you about," you are more likely to say, "What is it?"

Needless to say David is brilliant and I recommend you get his book: *Advertising Headlines that Make You Rich.*

When explaining things like benefits and features to the individual or group in writing or with the spoken word use short sentences and paragraphs when possible. Be sure to vary the length of sentences and paragraphs. Communicate with easy-to-understand words that hit an emotional "hot button." Save your "sophisticated" vocabulary for the pompous if you ever find yourself in front of one! Even then, you're still better off to keep it simple!

Remember this....

"If you confuse 'em, you lose 'em."

Jeff Paul, a brilliant marketer, said: "Communicate with

your prospect like he is Homer Simpson." In other words, keep it simple!

## A quick example of how a few words can make huge difference

I frequently help small and medium sized companies with their telephone procedures. It's amazing that a few simple adjustments can equal thousands of dollars to a company's bottom line. Here is an example.

I was working with a small company that needed to secure face-to-face meetings from their inbound phone calls. Basically, they did marketing to generate the calls but could not sell over the phone. They needed to have a rep meet face to face with the prospect. This company's service could not be sold based on price. The face-to-face meeting was the only way they could establish any value and subsequently make a sale to stay in business.

The goal was to give enough information over the phone to secure the special visit without making the caller feel as though the company was hiding anything. The phone script that they were using was good, except for one fatal flaw. After the visit was set, the caller would always say. "Now can you give me an idea of how much this is?"

The problem with answering the question was twofold: The salesperson was not able to establish enough value on the phone to justify the price and one of my rules is:

Never give a price until you have established a value. The other major problem was that the stats showed these callers were less likely to keep their appointments. The subconscious curiosity factor was gone.

Sounds like quite a conundrum huh? Here's what we did. We made a few very minor modifications to the entire script. Then we added one sentence that literally changed the fate of this company. After the "special visit" was secure we had the reps say; "Great, you're all set for Thursday at 6PM, I look forward to meeting you, and at this special time I'll be able to answer all of your questions in person, thanks for calling."

This worked like a charm and the company grew!

## Be Clear and Don't Assume

When I was operating my first business in South Philly, there was a guy named Tom who would help me out from time to time with odd jobs. One of the odd jobs I needed his help with was the distribution of fliers in some local grocery stores.

In South Philly, there's a small grocery store on every street corner. So naturally, not knowing much about fancy marketing or business strategies, I figured this would be a good strategy. These stores are sometimes referred to as "Mom and Pop" stores, but they all have different names: "Joe's Deli," or "South Philly Grocery" you get the idea.

The plan was simple. I excitedly told Tom that I needed him to go around to all of the "Mom and Pop" corner stores and talk to the shopkeepers and see if it would be okay to put fliers on the counter. From my experience, about 80% will have no problem and say "Sure!" I gave Tom a stack of fliers and said: "See ya in a few hours!"

He came back in less than an hour with a whole stack of fliers in his hand. Obviously there was a problem. I said, "Tom, what happened?" He said, "This seems like a great idea, but there is one major problem." "What is that?" "There's only one 'Mom and Pop' store and they can only take so many fliers." Puzzled, I then realized that he was actually right! In our area there was one corner store that was called "Mom and Pop" So he could only find one "Mom and Pop" store!

I get a good laugh whenever I tell this story, but the lesson is really twofold: Don't assume that your jargon will be picked up and understood by someone else. Then, be absolutely clear about your directions because giving directions to someone who is an employee, a co-worker, or just a guy named Tom who is helping you out is still persuasion!

Stay up on the latest (somewhat funny) "Street Smart Persuasion" stories. Go to www.askmiked.com and register for my e-zine.

## Street Smart Secret # 3- Put Everything In Terms of What It Means To Them

Remember, nobody cares about you and what you've accomplished! What you've accomplished does add credibility and this will get you further along. But, all they care about is what you can do for them. Every action has a self-serving purpose (even if folks don't admit it) and you need to make the people you are persuading understand what is in it for them.

Below are some statements you often see in marketing. The problem is that they really don't mean anything!

"We've been in business since 1978!"

"We are number one in our field."

"We use the highest quality Ingredients."

We – We – We .....Shut up!

Closing the loop is so important – Let me show you...

"We've been in business since 1978, therefore, you have peace of mind knowing that rock solid dependability and reliability is what you get with us."

"We have been given the prestigious (Whatever

Industry Award) by our customers because of the outstanding, 'get it done today' service that we offer."

"We use the highest quality ingredients free from (Something scary) so that you know your family's health is safe."

## Phrases that persuade in a group or one on one setting

1. And what this means to you (insert First Name) is....
2. How that affects you is...
3. Doing __ will result in _____ for you...
4. You'll also get...
5. You may be asking yourself...
6. How does that sound?
7. Here's what this means to you...
8. Here's how doing x will make you $y....
9. But wait, there's more!
10. And most importantly, here's why...
11. Is that the situation you find yourself in? Because if that's the case...
12. Doesn't that excite you?
13. Here's another thing....
14. But, this is just the beginning!
15. Fair enough?

Feel free to add more to this list and keep good records because sometimes we forget more than we know!

I find myself using these words and phrases at home and my wife will say, "Stop that!" Once you get to this point you know it has become natural.

# Street Smart Secret # 4- Truly Keep Their Best Interest in Mind and Give Them Some ROI

I totally believe the words of Kevin Hogan, author of, *The Psychology of Persuasion,* when he said, "It's easier to persuade someone who trusts and knows you really do have their best interest in mind."

ROI- "Return on Investment"

This relates back to "win-win" propositions and creating value for others. Everyone needs to get a return on his or her investment with you. If they don't, you'll quickly be out of the game. In my speaking and consulting business, my goal is for every company I work with or speak for to see a measurable return on their investment with me. If I train a sales team the next week they are out there being more persuasive and closing more sales – that's ROI!

It doesn't matter what your business is, you can easily give someone ROI in a few different ways.

## Be genuine

You cannot fake genuine sincerity. If you are not genuine, others will pick up on it with their gut feeling. When we fall victim to a con man, in most cases we went against our gut feeling. We're all programmed with a defense mechanism against folks who don't have our best interests in mind. Make sure you're not setting off the natural defenses of the people you're persuading. It's amazing, the wrong words or the wrong body language can cause someone to put their guard up.

I know you are genuine with your customers and clients, but also be sure to focus on them and block out other distractions! They know when you are checking email and multitasking, so stop!

## Show them the Quick Return

If your product or service can enhance someone's life, save her money or pay for itself with current or future income be sure to show them quickly how it will do so.

Structure your words so that within seconds of meeting them they will easily understand that talking with you further will be time well invested.

Get to the point and set goals for initial meetings. To paraphrase Dan Seidman of SalesAutopsy.com: Get to the point, your prospects are busy, gone are the days of looking on the office walls for something to chit chat about!

"Always keep in mind the person on the other side. If they don't feel like they have made a good deal you will lose in the end!"

# Street Smart Secret # 5-
# Balance The Two A's

Aggression & Agreeability

If you're tilted too far to either side, you'll lose your persuasive powers.

Too aggressive...You'll turn others off! This is true in business and personal relationships. When someone is in 'hot pursuit' we'll tend to duck and dodge until they back off.

Too agreeable...You fold easily! While plain vanilla has been the bestselling ice cream for many years, it's a risky strategy for anyone trying to build an organization, a business or persuade others.

Not everyone has or should agree with your viewpoint, nor should you care too much if they don't.

The funny thing is when you care, but not too much, you attract others to you and give yourself more leverage in the persuasive process.

I learned from James Malinchak to remember your "SW's" when it comes to persuading others...

"Some Will, Some Won't, So What!"

I offend people every day in some way. Everyone does not agree with everything I write or say. That's fine with me because the only people who have to like it are the folks that invest in my books, higher me to speak and count on me to train their sales people and help with their marketing. I'd suggest you develop the same attitude!

"Follow your prospect's mind. Let them do most of the talking. If they feel you are trying to push them they will shut                    you                    out."

## Street Smart Secret # 6- Give Them Time To Decompress: How To Say Goodbye to "We Need To Think It Over!"

You'll want to begin using this secret right away! Before we reveal it though, let me ask you a question.

What objection do you most despise? If you're like most of us, you've answered, "I hate when they want to think it over!" We all hate this one because it's so hard to wrap your hands around it. "I want to think it over" is like fog. Of course there are few things you can say after you hear this one that'll give you a prayer in the persuasive process. But, wouldn't life be so much better and wouldn't you be forever thankful that you read this book if you can make this problem disappear?

There really are two secrets to making this one go away forever. The first secret is to always bring it up to the person or group you are attempting to persuade early on in the process. You can say, "So how long have you been thinking about upgrading this phase of your company's operations?" If you are selling cars you can say, "How long have you been thinking about getting a Mercedes?" The key is to ask it early on in the interview and bring it up in the beginning of the presentation. In short, you should do this as part of your intelligence gathering! But this is not the secret I'm talking about!

The secret is much more powerful.

Now for the BIG secret to making "We need to think it over" go away forever...

You must give them time to decompress! Here's what I mean. We know that money, investment options and price must always be handled at the end of the presentation. Asking for a decision out of context or too early without establishing value will kill your chances of getting the "Yes" you need.

Here's what to do:

Break up your presentation into sections. Look for a smooth spot in the presentation that you can say; "Give me one second, I'll be right back in a couple minutes." The key is to build this in where it won't seem rude or be a disservice to the people you are influencing. If you are selling insurance, you can hit all of the emotional buttons you need to such as, fear of loss, love, family and financial security. Then, at the right moment, you basically pause and say, "This all makes sense so far, right? I'll be back in a second." Naturally, you've got to be smooth about it.

Once they have enough information (because you've already given it to them) they can do their thinking, talking and discussing right there. Remember though, you did not reveal the money part yet! What happens pretty much takes place at an unconscious level. Once you get back in the room they can't honestly say they want think it over. They can't, because when you are gone for the couple of minutes that's what they'll do! They'll huddle up, they'll discuss and they'll make a decision based on your presentation.

Here's the secret. You gave them time to decompress and they had a conversation in your absence that would have never taken place in your presence. To give credit where credit is due I learned this awesome technique from a gentleman named, Michael McNurney, he sells Long Term Care Insurance. When I learned it from him I adapted it to the business I was in at the time and it worked like a charm!

Now you can say goodbye to "We need to think it over." Go ahead, say goodbye!

"While the techniques of persuasion are important, it is the person behind them that does the business. It is the human power back of the techniques that will get the yes."

# Street Smart Secret # 7- Follow 3 Classic Formulas

I'm going to share with you three classic sales formulas that have stood the test of time. These formulas have stood the test of time because no matter what changes in the world, people are still the same.  All people make decisions the same way! Corporate executive or suburban housewife, we're all emotionally wired. Oh, By the way, people from different towns and regions are basically the same too. So no more excuses.

Persuasion has been around forever and these formulas aren't far behind. So let's explore...

1. Problem/Agitate/Solve

 Basically state a problem that the person you're persuading can identify with. Agitate it a little...Sort of like getting out your saltshaker and pouring some salt in the wound.  Solve it...But more importantly, show how what you have will solve the problem and make the pain go away!

 2. Before/ After

You've most likely seen infomercials offering fitness related products where all through the presentation you see evidence of the people who have used the products and lost weight. Think of the "before and after" success stories you've helped your customers achieve and use them in your presentation.

### 3. A.I.D.A. Attention, Interest, Desire, Action

Whenever you're speaking to a group of people or an individual make sure to get their attention very quickly. Do this by telling them what is in it for them. Gain interest by showing the folks that the benefits they came looking for are going to be fulfilled plus many more that they didn't expect. They will naturally begin to desire more of you based on what they've seen so far. Finally, call them to action by showing them how to get started and then simply asking them to do so.

Every presentation should follow one of these formulas or contain elements of all three.

Many "New Age" sales trainers who are really just trying to get you to believe that their new method is the best will falsely tell you that these formulas are outdated. These folks are just trying to sell books by preying on the fact that our society is obsessed with "New things." I guess they figure if they come up with some "New Method" they can get some attention – I guess it works. But let me ask you – do you want a rookie leading you in the championship game or an experienced all-star who has been there before? The above formulas are experienced all-stars.

# Street Smart Secret # 8- Become a Celebrity and an Expert through Writing and Speaking

People want to deal with celebrities and experts. Subconsciously, it's easier to persuade others if you are the expert or have some sort of celebrity status. No! You need not be someone with all kinds of fancy degrees to be an expert; of course having advanced degrees does help your status if you leverage them properly. And No! You need not be a movie star or athlete to be a celebrity.

When I first started in business when I was eighteen, I really had no clue how to write or give an effective presentation. One of my early mentors said on a cassette tape that speaking and writing are two of the most powerful skills in the business world.
He said, "If you can speak well and write well, you can write your own ticket and the world is yours." Makes sense, doesn't it? His suggestion was to write at least one page per day no matter what.

You should also be practicing writing information. What kind of information? The kind that shows your customers and clients how they can benefit from your service. You need to practice writing practical 'how to' material that links back to your product, service, and business. By becoming a pretty good writer through daily practice, you end up becoming a respected expert in your field or local community where you are doing business. The easiest place practice is on your business (or personal) blog.

Just remember all of your writing should tie back in to your business so people then seek you out as the trusted expert. If you want to write the next great American novel, go for it, but don't expect it to do much for your local plumbing business. But a pamphlet titled: "Little Known Plumbing Problems that Are Draining Your Bank Account" where you talk about how overlooked plumbing issues can cost the prospect a fortune will help your business.

You're not trying to win a prize, you're just becoming competent so you can set yourself apart from your competitors and become a celebrity in your market.

If you're thinking; "I can't write" or "It'll take too long!" Remember this:

Your competition is saying the same thing. So it would be a good idea for you to take action.

It's not hard! Think about and write down all of the questions your prospects ask you. Then, simply turn that into a report or article. Of course, you will tilt the report or article in your favor without making it a blatant sales pitch. What is great is that the reader will come to the natural conclusion that you can solve their problems.

When I work with business owners one of the areas we focus on is the "expert position." I help them construct what I call "informational persuasion." This helps them attract clients rather than go on the hunt for prospects.

## Speaking

Speaking with large groups can provide you with massive amounts of leverage. If you can be in front of fifty, one hundred, or even more people at one time who have a need for your products and services you've really hit a home run.

The idea is not to get up there and say; "Is this thing on, can everyone hear me?" or "I'd like to thank, blah, blah and blah for having me, let's give them a hand."

NO! Your job is to speak, to persuade your audience to the natural conclusion that they need what you've got. This is called platform persuasion.

A good speaker will give a sixty to ninety-minute talk packed with solid useful information. They will reach their audience emotionally through relevant stories, humor, and body language. They will identify a particular problem that the audience may have and give them a good, simple solution for solving the problem.

A good platform persuader will bring up any possible obstacles that their audience may have to their proposition and answer them immediately. They will keep the audience entertained and wanting more throughout the entire presentation. They will cause the audience to want more of them, be it through products, services or membership. And finally, they'll tell the audience what they need to do to take action.

Some people seem to do this naturally. However, selling from the platform is a learned skill that should not be left to chance. Experience and the help of an qualified coach can help you here too. You can trust me when I tell you that if you've ever purchased something at an event or seminar it was entirely planed from minute to minute.

Here's an outline to follow so you can craft a persuasive talk.

Start with a "Grabber." I learned this from Paul Hartunian, the guy who actually sold the Brooklyn Bridge in the early 1980's (When I was just a little guy). The grabber is designed to grab the audience and force them to pay attention. The best grabbers are the ones that tell the audience why they need to listen to you.

After your grabber, you'll need to build a little initial rapport with your group. Do this by telling a short story. Show proof and credentials. Maybe numbers, testimonials, or a description of how you use what you're talking about.

Show more details of how you can help the audience.

Make a transition with another story. Wrap up your presentation by directing the audience on what they need to do to get more of you.

Don't overlook this opportunity. If you want to become a better speaker simply join Toastmasters International. You can learn, practice and master your presentation skills in one of their clubs.

The Internet really does makes writing, speaking and communicating to your market easy. You can become the star of your own video or audio blog. You can start a written blog to keep your customers and prospects up to date.

# Street Smart Persuasion Meets Academic Research.

This bonus section contains the exact transcript of an interview I did with Robert Levine. Robert Levine has been researching the field of persuasion for more than twenty years.

In this eye-opening and fun Mid-Book Bonus you'll discover more persuasive secrets and see how everything we have covered and will cover in the rest of this book is proven in the world of academics, but works where you need it most – on the street.

Mike Dolpies:

On the phone with me today I have Robert Levine and he is a professor of *psychology* and former *Associate Dean of The College of Science and Mathematics at California State University of Fresno* where he has won awards for both his teaching and research.

He is a fellow in the *American Psychological Association.* In 2007 he was both named "*Outstanding Teacher of the Year*" by the *Western Psychological*

*Association* and received the *Provost Award* for "*Teacher of the Year*" at the *California State University of Fresno*. He has published many articles and professional journals as well as articles and trade publications such as *Discover, American Demographics, The New York Times* and *American Scientist*.

His recent book "*The Power of Persuasion: How We're Bought and Sold*" published by *John Wiley & Sons* in 2003 has been translated in to seven languages. There is an updated paperback version, that was published recently in 2006 and I would encourage everybody to go to Amazon or wherever books are sold and grab that book. It is a real treat to be talking to you today Bob and really appreciate it. How are you?

Robert Levine:

I am doing fine mike. How are you?

Mike Dolpies:

I am doing wonderful. I know you have been researching the field of persuasion for many years from the academic side. My Book is called *Street Smart Persuasion* and in it I talk about the real life, practical side of ethical persuasion. I was hoping to get your perspective on the persuasive process. You have studied advertising, one-to-one scenarios and influencing groups of people. Is that okay with you to cover those grounds?

Robert Levine:

Sure.

Mike Dolpies:

Alright then let us get going. In your book, you talk about the illusion of invulnerability. Can you tell us little bit about that?

Robert Levine:

Yes. This notion of kind of normal-abnormal abnormality, if you can excuse the psychobabble from a social psychologist, in my field what we found is there are number of ways of thinking and acting that are normal in the sense that they are a norm that most people do, the majority of people do it but a number of these can be destructive, personally destructive, destructive to other people.

One of the norms that comes out of this notion of personal invulnerability, which says that bad things are more likely to happen to other people than to ourselves, and it comes out in health psychology - there is a huge amount of data showing that. If you ask people what are the chances that you are going to contract a certain disease compared to as opposed to the likelihood that other people your same age, gender is going to contract it, there is this overwhelming bias towards believing that it is more likely to happen to other people.

The statistical inanities - and it does not matter - it goes across intelligence, it goes across age and such and it makes sense in a certain way, I mean it is self-protective.

We do not want to go out, we do not want to live our days thinking that terrible things are going to happen to us. It is no way to live one's life. But on the other hand what we find is that it can leave us more vulnerable than we were in the first place and to bring it back to persuasion this is I think exhibit A of this, because what we found - we have done our own studies where we asked people how likely are you to be duped by another person, how vulnerable are you to conman, how much do you know about persuasion process, how intelligent, how much street sense you have - and there is a vast tendency for people to, everybody to think that they are more savvy than and less likely to be duped and taken advantage of than other people, which is again it's fine, it's a comforting notion, but what is really the killer in when it comes to persuasion is that there are people who are clever enough to know that this is one of your weak spots, that it is one of those hot buttons, that if they can play to this belief that you are invulnerable and they kind of massage your ego and then come in under your radar and take advantage of you.

So it is kind of the worst, it is one of the most vulnerable situation because you have people who are exploiting that and you see it on so many levels and you certainly see it with the fast talkers and the really good sales people who come at you. They just come in to your radar. They do not look like sales people; they are just your pals. They just sidle up next to you and then they go in for the kill.

You also see it in more organized ways. If you watch good advertising, clever advertising, they do not play you like a dummy. They are kind of winking at you all the time like they understand that you are above all this. But in the meantime you walk away wearing the *Budweiser* hat. Anyway that is a long answer to a very simple question.

Mike Dolpies:

All of my listeners and clients, we all make our living with persuasion. We have members, we have our own clients and we have to do our best to get people to (in an ethical way of course) to get people to give up money in so many ways, and the reason why I brought that up is because I wanted to kind of jolt a few of the listeners at the same time to say, 'What's he going against everything that he teaches? Is he exposing us for what we are?' And that is why I wanted to ask you that question first.

One thing I know, I am sure you do, and all our listeners know is that there is going to be a certain amount of people out there, the vast majority of the general public is never going to know Bob's research, never going to read Bob's book, never going to read my book, never going to get any of what I am saying so they are just never going to be aware of this kind of stuff, but how do we as business owners ethically, knowing what you just told us, how do we ethically persuade using this training?

Robert Levine:

> Yes. As you know as well as I do Mike that is a really difficult question. There is a chemistry there, there is a big grey zone that is very hard to grapple with. As you are describing it for yourself as somebody who is coming at it more from the sales part, I grapple with it in the same way for somebody who is coming at it from the consumer part.
>
> I am a college professor. I am not a salesperson so what I am doing is trying to orient it towards the consumer but nonetheless; all that either of us can do is come up with ideas.
>
> All we can do is paint the psychology and the psychology is either correct or it is incorrect and I have a tendency in my field to do experimental studies, to do empirical work and we can find that what this type of salesperson or this type of message or this type of salesperson delivering this type of message to this type of consumer is going to be more effective than something else. And then again I mean I can conclude that this is what consumers should be watching out for but of course, the other conclusion is that this is what people who are in sales and marketing, should be thinking about

when they are presenting their message.

So now the question becomes, as you say, how do we do it, how do we embrace this, how do we embrace the correct information and how do we do it in an ethical way? And I think both of us pretty much know the answer to that. We know when we are doing wrong. We know when we are manipulating. We know when we are selling people things that they really do not want and that they are really not going to need and that they really do not want and there are other times when the person tells you that they do not want it when you have sensed that well maybe if I educate you and maybe if I put it all on the table in a way, then maybe you are going to see that hey here is an option I never thought about.

It is interesting to look back on marketing and advertising back a hundred years ago. If you read the kind of statements that people are making and not just marketers but you read what politicians say, the people saw advertising and marketing as kind of a pro-social message. It was an educational message to let you know what is available and what is out there and they were big reasons but there is a wishy-washy answer from an academic but you know we academics are like that.

Mike Dolpies:

> The main reason why I was really thrilled when you agreed to do this was knowing and doing my own research, it is great to have a little bit of controversy for one, but knowing both sides of the coin that is pretty powerful as well. Would you agree with that?

Robert Levine:

> Yes. It is very powerful. You mean both sides of the coin being, understanding it from the receiver and from the passer?

Mike Dolpies:

> Yes.

Robert Levine:

> Absolutely. and I know it also. One of the things that I get to in the book, in "The Power of Persuasion" is the fact that I can sit back as an ethically driven professor and criticize the world of people who are trying to make money from other people. But I am using persuasion all day long. I mean I am using it in my book I am setting it out, in my classes I am setting it

out, I'm using the same kind of principle. I am not just putting up a billboard that says, "social psychology is worth knowing".

What I do is I come in gently; I try to establish a rapport. I am really doing my own sort of, as they say in the sales industry, I am doing my own meet and greet. I am selling myself. I am selling a product. I build things slowly. I do not give people more than they can handle at any point and I try to help them draw conclusions themselves. And one of the questions that I try to pose when I am teaching it is how I am different from an exploitive - I do not want to point finger at anybody but certainly used car dealers are an interesting example– how am I different from it and the best answer that I can come up with is that I do not have a double agenda, that I really am there to try to empower other people. While when I took a job as a used-car dealer, when I was writing the book I know it was a very different situation. As you pointed out I think and I think you know it from firsthand experience, knowing both sides can be very powerful. It can be informative, educational, it gives you a sense of what is going on with other people and it also allows you to do it responsibly.

Mike Dolpies:

> Study the book of human nature, the answers are written on its pages right?

Robert Levine:

> Yes. That is right. Yes.

Mike Dolpies:

> What you said, I just want to point out a couple of things for our listeners. One... what you said about having the agenda of really not having a double agenda... that fits our listeners and I hope that everyone was really paying attention to the way you ran down how you go about this process in your life, because the way you ran through that and concluded was the exact steps that I think a lot of our clients should be taking. I hope that they go back and rewind and then listen to what you said there.

Robert Levine:

> When I wrote "*The Power of Persuasion*" one of the things that I did, I mean I have been studying persuasion for a long time and as an academic I know the research

very well but I wanted to go out and try to do it.

So I went out and took a couple of jobs. I took a job selling knives, I took a job, I went through the training with Cutco and then I took a couple of jobs as a used-car salesman and it was fascinating. It was so interesting to watch people who are actually doing the things that I was talking about.

What really got me after a while was after I understood the process - and I have it as kind of a ten-step process with all sorts of psychologies, psychology in the raw that just wrapped through this process – that I found that the same psychology, pretty much the same psychology, pretty much those ten-steps could be applied to the persuasion that I use in trying to give people a liberalized education and then from there I found that I could apply it so many different things.

I started studying cults, I find they are doing the same thing, traditional religion are doing it, politicians are doing it, people who are running presidential campaigns are doing it. I think it is a question of form over content. The form seems to be pretty much the same. I think effective persuasion, the process of effective persuasion is pretty similar all across the board. It is almost like there is some *Darwinian* grammar going on there. How it is applied and what the goals are what the end points are, that is a whole other story.

Mike Dolpies:

It actually brings us to a question I have written down here because in your research you went through a lot of jobs. Did the companies know what you were doing?

Robert Levine:

No. You wanted to hear something funny. Listen I am a college professor, I mean I am an academic from way back. I mean I deal with books and ideas, numbers, and writers. So when I went out to take these jobs I did not know what I should do, how much should I tell them? Nobody cared. Nobody cared.

First I went to Cutco, I went through the knives and they asked me what do I do and I told them I was a college professor. Nobody asked me what are you doing? It was the realization pretty quickly that it does not matter who goes through that process because they are exploiting each of the salesmen as middle people. It is not just a commission process but it is a way of getting to all the people that those sales people are close to so they do not care. They figured out I am older and I probably know people with money so I was fine so there were no questions there.

When I went for the car dealership I told them. I was doing it in my hometown and I certainly was not going to be completely fraudulent about it so I told them I was a college professor, I told them the truth about that I have been teaching this stuff for years and I wanted to apply it which was all true. The only thing I did not tell them was that I was writing a book. In fact, when they asked me for names of people that I could use for references I gave them some of my colleagues and there wasn't any problem there. It did not seem to matter.

Mike Dolpies:

I know you have been through some different training programs in the process. Now what were your biggest - based on the fact that you were not going into these training programs as somebody who had a blank slate. I guess that is the best way to put it. I started a business when I was 18, I opened my first martial arts studio, I can say without any shame that I started with a blank slate. So you definitely were not starting with a blank slate based on everything you said you knew. So what were your biggest breakthroughs and takeaways from the experience of going through training programs and then subsequently working I guess to use the word 'selling'?

Robert Levine:

That is a good question. I will take down the second question first because I think I have not been asked that before but it elicits a pretty strong response and that is that in terms of putting it into practice what I found very quickly was that there was a certain ability that I lack.

I will give you an example. When I was selling cars, as you know there is a lot of downtime for car salesmen and the people were very nice and they were very friendly and they kind of saw me as the new kid on the block and I guess I certainly did not look like a threat to anybody, trust me I did not look like a threat to anybody and so they were kind of showing me around and showing me the ropes and this one guy, he watches me do a meet and greet and I began my meet and greet the way I would meet and greet anybody that I meet, which is I try to be friendly but I do not know the person so I do it in kind of a mild way and hopefully they will get to know each other a little bit better and it will build into some sort of closeness and the guy he turns to me after it is over and he says, "That is not the way you do it". He says you look like you did not even care and he shows me how he does it.

He goes to a complete stranger who he knows mistrusts him completely and he mistrusts the person completely. One of the things one car salesman told me, he says, "Here is all you have to know about the car sales process is all customers are liars and all salesmen are cheats". This is the attitude that many of these folks are going into and certainly new customers are. So he goes up to this person like he is his best friend. I can hardly even say it on the phone and this is what my point is that I can hardly imitate it I should say, 'Hi! How are you? I am so and so and welcome to so and so motors,' and he says try it and I went to try to do it and the words got caught in my throat. I could not do it. I was not able to do it.

I could not project that way. I guess that

was one of the great insights was that some people have a certain talent. It is almost a drama sort of a talent and I could be cynical about it but on the other hand I could say to you that knowing what it is like to be a lecturer that I know that I put on an act when I am lecturing. And I think the realization that some folks have a real talent for the sales process.

The other thing that I found and I guess this would be an important message as I am speaking to people who are on the sales end right now, is that I found that when I was selling that I many ways I was the wrong person to be there for somebody who wanted to buy. When people are going around they were looking to buy cars and all that I could do, I just wanted to tell them save your money. You just told me how much money you have, why do you want to waste money on another car, it is going to look just like the other car in a little while? Go get yourself an education or something! And what I was doing was that I was depriving them of the pleasure of what they wanted.

I sold one car grand total, so I do not mean to generalize this so far but I remember that person who bought it, what they wanted me to say afterwards was that you have just made the best buy in the world. You have just changed your life around, everything, the entire quality of your life is going to pick up, and I am just looking at them like, you know, get a life okay, buy something more substantial and I think that is the part of the role of a good salesperson is to make it the experience that the customer wants it to be.

Mike Dolpies:

Yes. I think it was Tony Allessandra's Platinum Rule, "Do unto others as what they want to be done unto".

Robert Levine:

Oh very good, very good. I had not heard that before. I like that.

Mike Dolpies:

Yes. I think we as marketers, salespeople, and business owners we definitely make our living– I do not want to use the phrase "talking people in to things" – but certainly not talking people out of things.

You have a steady job as a professor whereas the salesman is out there every day. I have another colleague, his name is Ben Gay,III he's got one of the bestselling publications on closing sales and he says about his clients: "If they do not make a sale today they do not eat tonight." So certainly the opposite of your position, right?

Robert Levine:

That is right. I have that luxury that I have a steady pay check coming in and I fully appreciate that and I fully appreciate that difference I mean I have also made it a point in times of my life to pull myself in a position where I had to live on my wits for times and several years ago - some of my earlier work is on cross-cultural psychology- I wrote a book based on those experiences when I traveled around the world for a year. And I liked that. It was really important to me to get that steady paycheck out of the way and to just try to live by my wits for a year and it makes me appreciate what I saw.

Especially on the car lot when I am watching people who are out there working very long hours on really not very substantial commission with a lot of competition not only of course dealership but of course sales people. And to watch what folks had to do and certainly there is an inclination there to just grab what you can with no thoughts about the consequences to other people and there were some levels that I saw people operating that I have no question that I do not want to sound smarty about it but that I completely disapproved of what they did. People who are lying, they were just plain lying and playing tricks on other people. But then there were the other ones who would, there were a number of other people who really enjoyed the persuasion process, who were just fighting tooth and nail to bring people over to their side, to maximize their profits and they were doing it certainly without fraud and also with great professionalism.

Mike Dolpies:

Well hey just to go back a few sentences that we are definitely not going to question your ability to live on your wits. I think your research and everything you have done is just great, so I hope you do not take it that way. Real quick to sum up on this particular section, based on all the training programs you went through what would you say was one of the most effective process that you were trained on.

Robert Levine:

> That I can answer easily. It was the training in selling cars and mostly I would say, well I could go on for a while about it, but I guess what comes to my mind mostly is that the slowly escalating commitments. The notion of, to use the sales term, of getting a foot in the door and once having that foot in the door, escalating the customer's commitments in multiple steps, never asking more than the customer was willing to give, and a number of sales people I spoke to there said that you cannot skip a step, you cannot let the customer skip a step or else it is going to come back to bite you in the end. I think that maybe a bit of an over generalization but I think there is a lot of truth to it.
>
> The words that I would use in psychology to describe that is what we found in study after study is that once somebody makes a small commitment, it is less likely that they are going to say no to a larger commitment. In our field what we'll often do is show the terrible things that we can get folks to do. We have the shock studies where people thought they were given 450 volts to complete strangers, and when people walk in and they observe and say how can people be

so cruel but we find it that the key is not asking people to skip the 450 volts it is asking people to give 15 volts and once people have said yes to the 15 volts it becomes less and less likely that they are going to say no as the commitments escalate and I am not trying to mix the two but I think it is that same grammar, the notion of moving slowly and patiently.

Mike Dolpies:

If you were to sum up what would you say the real key to effective one-on-one persuasion would be?

Robert Levine:

Well I think that one of them is never pushing too hard. Of course it depends on the individual that you are working with. Some people you would want to push a little bit harder than other people but for the most part never pushing too hard, never pushing too fast, giving people their space and trying to let them see what it is and being clear about what it is that you could show them that you really want to educate them as to at least present it as an education as to what you have to offer.

Mike Dolpies:

> Now if we were to transition little bit and talk about the marketing and advertising side of things. What did you find to be some of the most common principles used in marketing and advertising as opposed to – we just talked a lot about one-on-one side of things, but now when we are talking about broad, communicating with masses at one time, in your studies what have you found were the most effective and most commonly used principles?

Robert Levine:

> Yes. I want to say a couple of things here and I do not think if this going to answer the way that you are interested so we can come back to it if you want but two things that come to mind very strongly. One is when it comes to marketing and advertising is that we did a study where we asked people, 'Does advertising work?' And most people say that advertising is effective.
>
> Then we asked people, 'Does advertising work on you?' And almost everybody says, "No it does not work on me".  And this is just better than average of that and this

illusion of invulnerability that we talked about and to understand that marketers and advertisers understand this they know about this and so they know that especially if they know that the demographics they are selling to are educated people, they are going to play and exploit this illusion of invulnerability. There are going to try to let you know that well 'I am not really an advertiser, I am really an educator, or I am going to present it as news or I am going to present it as fact.' So that would be one aspect I think of this advertising and marketing.

The other thing that I would say about advertising is that was very educational for me when I realized this is that it used to be when I was growing up that I was always warned about how advertising is all lies, that you cannot trust advertising and then when I started to study most of the especially the mass media, advertising that we see, I saw that there are not any lies there because there isn't any information being communicated.

The big products do not talk about, they do not say that Coca-Cola has some kind of characteristic that it does not really have, that it has some kind of chemistry that it does not have. It is all theatre. It is all roles. The Coca-Cola can is there and the question becomes to the advertisers, 'What are we going to surround it with, are we going to surround it with big professional athletes with hearts gold or we are going to surround it with skate boarders or we are going to surround it with people who are holding hands singing *We are the World*.'

It is very interesting to watch when you start to key in on this, you start to key in what these products are doing spending these fortunes in advertising and never really saying anything about the product, just trying to present a drama with the hope that some niche of their consumer community are going to choose to be part of this drama. I have a hunch that did not answer the question the way you wanted to put in the beginning but...

Mike Dolpies:

We appreciate that. I think it makes perfect sense. It is more of showman ship. Do you see any big disparities between you know - using Coca-Cola as an example obviously that is an example of a brand-type marketing, using millions and millions of dollars, but did you study and smaller type of business? My world is direct response type advertising type of marketing? Did you study any of that?

Robert Levine:

I do not know if I have too much on the way of insight there. What I can say, if you would excuse me a little bit of psychology jargon right now, when we talk about the methods of advertising, really the methods of persuasion but it applies so much to advertising and marketing. You talk about the jargon is "the central route versus the peripheral route" to persuasion and I will throw away the jargon now and just talk about it.

The difference between on the one hand presenting fact and information, objective information in a logical, sequential way, so trying to influence people with real information and really try to give an education versus giving peripheral sorts of information, the idea of whatever you are going to say, throw in another dog and a woman in a bikini kind of idea, and I think what my own observation - and I have not done this empirically - but my own observation is that when we get to smaller businesses that one needs clearly to focus on more objective information. It is certainly not enough to just present sort of a drama that people are going to walk into. Often also of course it is that link for respectability, not respectability but for trustworthiness.

What we found is that, I mean the kind of person, the main sources and the communicator that people tend to respond to is authority and expertise. People have real information and then second is trustworthiness, kind of as a moral dimension, the kind of person you feel is not going to do you wrong, and then the third one which really makes no sense at all for most business arrangements but is maybe the most critical to most people is likeability, 'Do you like that salesperson?'

**Mike Dolpies:**

Now that is totally congruent to what we actually go over with our clients so that is great. Nice validation there.

**Robert Levine:**

Well both ways. You see for me I have got the data but then I need the validation of the people who are actually doing it.

Mike Dolpies:

Yeah, you got it anytime you want it.

Robert Levine:

Laughs.

Mike Dolpies:

Hey real quick before we change gears again, a lot of times marketers and advertisers they and even myself, we employ scarcity. What were some of your findings on scarcity and did you make any findings, where it was blatantly clear that 'hey this is B.S.'? Or was it, 'Well, wait a minute this might only be around for a couple of minutes here. I better snag one of these up.'

Robert Levine:

Right. Right.

Mike Dolpies:

Is that a question you can answer or not?

Robert Levine:

Yes. Well sure. I can certainly answer it in

kind of a general way. This is another one of those phrases where it is normal for people to react to feeling that something is not going to be there for a long time. This colleague by name of Robert Cialdini talks about the rule of scarcity that the less available it is the more we want it and the analysis of advertising showed that scarcity is most often used, almost slogans only three days left, clearance sale and such, and people do react to it. There is absolutely no question that people react to it. It goes back to being a kid. Anybody who has children knows what happens if you walk into the store and tell your child, you can have anything except for that flavor. That is one that we want.

Mike Dolpies:

Goes back to Adam and Eve. Right?

Robert Levine:

Yes. I think probably so. We don't have the data but I think you are right on that one.

Mike Dolpies:

Okay. That certainly is more validation there. No doubt about it. I'll change gears one more time before we finish up and real quick, will you tell everybody where your book is available?

Robert Levine:

Oh sure. I appreciate that. The name of the book is "*The Power of Persuasion: How We're Bought and Sold*" and the easiest place is to get it online. It is published by Wiley, it is available there, it is in some bookstores, but the best, I would just go to Amazon, it is cheaper on Amazon also and if you want any more information about it or if you want to see anything more about the kind of work that I have been doing, I have a website, it is www.boblevine.net, easy to find.

Mike Dolpies:

Okay. Great. Many of our listeners they are responsible for influencing, persuading larger groups of customers, members, and clients. What in your research, and this a fascinating part in your book, what in your research have you found to be – and we'll talk about both sides of the coin here - is the effective side or the person influencing and the defensive side or the person who might be subject to the technique.

Robert Levine:

> Sure. Well we'll get into a long list here and we have talked a lot about it in the last few minutes. Certainly this maybe just reframing of some of the things that we have said, that we have been talking about already but one of the keys I think for most people is that people are sophisticated, customers are sophisticated and wary and we have such a long history of sales people coming after us, advertisers coming after us that we screen out everything, we filter out everything and as soon as somebody is recognized as a sales person unless it is a product that we are actively seeking ourselves, people tend not to listen at all and what I found is that one of the keys to a salesperson getting a foot in the door is not to appear to be like a quote salesperson.
>
> I have it easy. In my field, when I walk into the classroom people are not looking at me like a salesperson, so there is a certain level of trust that is there already. For most of the people listening to this program I do not think that you could say the same thing unless you have a personal referral but as soon as it moves anywhere in the vicinity of cold call it becomes that much of a problem. And I think that is

one of the keys is to present oneself as being closer to what my job is, it is being an educator, presenting the information as education, presenting it as perhaps news, as if that is the kind of field that you are in.

At the same time, as we talked about in these last few minutes is to do it with some responsibility so not to fraudulently present yourself, not to do some king of stealth marketing like these folks that are now hanging around Starbucks with products that they are making believe they are using for themselves and wait for somebody to walk up and say something about it. But to let people know that yes this is what I do for a living and hey you want to hear me out and I have some information and now you know somebody you can turn to if you want some more information. I know that is easier said than done when you are hustling from morning until night but I guess I like to think of it that way.

Mike Dolpies:

And I think if I were to sum it up I would say that is the most important principle - not coming off as a seller. As business owners there are ways for all of us to put ourselves closer to your position and I know it is possible and sometimes we help our clients to do so. It is great that you can validate that and to let you know our validation is that it works. Hey what do you think overall the people with good intentions and their actual high moral standards?  Do you think they come out on top most of the time in the field of persuasion?

Mike Dolpies:

Well hey like I said this was really a great opportunity and I really appreciate you coming along and taking your valuable time.  It is been a very eye-opening, insightful, and it is great to get the insights of someone in your position who has done years and years of research and teaching and actually applying.  So we really do appreciate it and one more time just want to sum up your website and you're the book again real quick?

Robert Levine:

Yes sure.  Well if anybody would like to see my website it is www.boblevine.net and there is ways to contact me if you like and the name of the book is "*The Power of Persuasion: How We're Bought and Sold*" published by Wiley and Sons and the cheapest place to get it I think is

Amazon.

Mike Dolpies:

Great. And you are still at California State University of Fresno?

Mike Dolpies:

Thanks so much. Take care.

# Street Smart Secret # 9- Always Leave Them Wanting More

In every situation you want to leave the folks wanting more of you and looking forward to the next time they will see you.

Put yourself in a child's shoes for a moment. They have short memories, they live in the now. A child can have a totally boring time all day at school. But, if the teacher does something really special for the kids before they leave you can rest assured that when they get home they'll be smiling and telling mom what a great day they had.

End your meetings on a positive note.

End all transactions with a "wow" factor.

Ask good questions in conversations with your prospects and let them talk. This will cause them to feel validated and cared for. They will want more of those feelings and more of you.

Study the entertainment and media industry, and you'll see how they make good use of hooks and cliff-hangers. When you set a visit to talk to someone let them know a few bullet points of what you'll be covering, example:

"Mr. Jones you are all set for 7PM Monday, when we meet we're going to talk about the three mistakes 90% of Americans make when planning for retirement, the two ways you can save more now, without, changing your lifestyle and the secret to saving for your child's college education, tax free."

This not only helps you to look more professional, but puts your presentation into persuasive language that causes the prospect to want more.

These strategies also work when trying to stimulate repeat business. I'm sure your business relies on repeat customers, right? Heck, even the funeral business does. And how do you get a repeat customer? Give them a reason to want more. I remember when I was between the ages of ten and twelve - six people in my family past away. Guess what, two funeral homes handled the six arrangements. I'm not saying that my family left there thinking they couldn't wait until the next person died! It was the trust that had been built up and the "wow factor" that led my family back.

# Street Smart Secret # 10- Easily Get Others to Help You

I advise everyone I speak with that's in business to read a great book by Robert Cialdini called *Influence, Science and Practice.* This book is the true bible for anyone looking to understand the science of influence in more depth.

Anyway, one of his principles is called "Social Proof." It basically states that all human beings validate things based on what others are doing.

"Must be good, the place is packed!"

"John's family is doing it, must be OK!"

Unfortunately, it can work for the negative too - just think of teenage peer pressure. I grew up in a tough inner city neighborhood. Believe me, the real tough kids are the ones who go against the crowd.

**For Your Business the Best Validation Comes in the Form of Testimonials.**

**Here's how you can get testimonials, FAST!**

When someone gives you a compliment about your product or service, say the following...

"Wow! I love hearing great feedback, can you do me favor?" Let them answer, "sure" and then say, "Would you mind if I used your feedback to help others who are looking for information?" They'll say "of course not!" You then take their picture and summarize their feedback for them and have them sign off on it.

I learned this technique from Bill Glazer, who is the president of Glazer-Kennedy Insider's Circle and one of the most in demand marketing consultants in the world.

A few hints.

Make them specific. Who they are, and what town they live in. You must include their full name and picture. Let just initials, as in "It was great", Joe T. warn you of a scam!

## How to spot a "B.S." testimonial!

I once saw a testimonial that read: *"I made $60,000 in six months, thanks for everything!" – B.S. Davis.*

Please make sure your testimonials give the full name of the person, their location and their picture when possible!

Make them "result specific" or have them overcome a concern. Make sure the testimonial gives details… "I made $x in three months using _____'s program!" "I was concerned about ____, but once I got going I realized that _____ was not a big deal."

Be very sure to get testimonials where there is common ground. The people you are persuading must be able to say to themselves, "Those people are just like me, if they can do it, so can I."

Using testimonials is extremely valuable to anyone in the game of persuasion. The biggest hang up most people have is their ability to collect them. Not anymore.

Are you enjoying this book so far? It's pretty easy to read and has given you some great ideas so far right?

Well, do me favor...

Go to Amazon.com and write me a glowing review of this book!
To show my appreciation I'll send a limo to your house to take you to your favorite restaurant! Just Kidding! Seriously, you wouldn't mind giving me a great review would you?

"Study your prospects. Learn to read the book of human nature. The formula for success is written on its pages.

# Street Smart Secret # 11- Don't Bet Against the "Fiddle Theory"

You're wondering, "What's the fiddle theory and whatever it is, why shouldn't I bet against it?" So let me define it for you real quick. The Fiddle Theory States, "The longer you allow someone to fiddle around with a deal, the less likely it is to close." We can use the word "deal" interchangeably with the word "decision."

Of course, I need always give credit where credit is due. I first read and leaned the fiddle theory in Robert Ringer's bestselling book, *"To Be or Not To Be Intimidated."* In the book, Mr. Ringer told of his first hand experiences as a young real estate broker. He watched the fiddle theory destroy countless deals he had worked on for a long time.

We need to understand that ethical persuasion lives and dies on timing and emotions. Positive emotions need to be leveraged and capitalized on if you are going to persuade others to your cause.

The longer someone has to make a decision, the longer they will fiddle around and put it off.

Don't misunderstand me either! I'm not saying that you need to be Mr. or Ms. "High Pressure Sales." What I'm saying is that you need to use your persuasive skills to lead someone to make a decision sooner rather than later. People do not "think it over."

When a meeting planner inquires about booking me to speak or a sales manager wants to bring me in for a day to train their people, I let them know that they should book the date while they have me on the phone. The reality is that the date may not be available if they wait too long to book it. I am not being high pressure. I'm just being honest. If they fiddle around with the decision we both lose. They miss out some valuable information that will help their company and I miss the business and the opportunity to make a difference for them. Plus they called me, I didn't call them.

# Street Smart Secret # 12- Little Yes's Equal Big Results- How to Profit from The Yes Momentum.

Before we dive into exploring the yes momentum what I will quickly do is sum it up for you...

The basic rule that governs this theory is the old sales gem that says... *Why tell something, when you can ask it.* When trying to gain yes momentum that one statement is gospel.

My little ones use this powerful persuasive principle often. Here's an example.

Julia loves to where "dress up" clothes. What amazes me is that the kid will be uncomfortable if her sweat pants are up too high or her socks are too thick. Yet, she'll want to lounge around in a princess costume or last year's Christmas dress all day.

One Saturday morning, when she was four, she got the urge to put on the previous year's Christmas dress. My wife figured that she only had a few months left before the dress would no longer fit her, so she gave in and let her put it on.

When she was younger she needed a good thirty minutes awake before she could eat her breakfast; it's just how her stomach was wired. After a few minutes, Jamie called her into the kitchen to eat her cereal. Jamie met some resistance when she told her to take her Christmas dress off and put her pajamas back on to eat. I guess Jamie didn't feel like adding the dress to the dry cleaning pile that week. Eventually Julia complied and put her pajamas back on to eat breakfast. Julia's employment of the "Yes Momentum" came at lunchtime.

It was time for lunch and Julia was still in her Christmas dress. Her lunch request was grilled cheese. I called her in and before I could tell her to take the dress off and put her pajamas back on to eat lunch she said; "Daddy, grilled cheeses are not that messy, they are neat right?" I knew exactly what she was up to! I said; "Yes they are neat, you're right."

Her goal was simple. She wanted to wear her dress while eating her lunch. She knew that if she got me to agree that "grilled cheeses were a neat food," I'd have no reason to make her take off the dress and wear her pajamas to eat lunch. Because she used the "Yes Momentum", she got to eat lunch in her dress of choice.

Naturally the questions you ask will be the ones that the person you're persuading can answer "YES!" to. So why is it so important to gain the yes momentum and how can you do it? Let's explore...

Never forget it - yes is the single most powerful word

you can hear in persuasion. Yes has to come before you get paid, there's just no way around it. Yes is what puts everyone in a positive frame of mind. Little yeses lead to big yeses and the total of all the yeses lead to you ringing the register and helping someone else do something that will truly benefit them and you.

 Whether you're in a group or one to one setting you need to get a bunch of yeses. Your prospects need to say yes to answer one of your pre-arranged questions. They need to say yes inside their own heads as you demonstrate how they will achieve the benefits they are searching for. All this establishes a great momentum as you finish up and begin your closing sequence. Let's explore...

## How to get Yeses

The best way to get yeses is to answer *with* the group or individual you're attempting to persuade. In a one-to-one setting get in the habit of nodding your head as you ask questions you want a yes for. When attempting to get yeses from a group, simply answer first and out loud. Only do this after you've grabbed their attention with a good benefit oriented-statement, established some rapport and built some creditability.

The yes momentum will carry you a long way, so always let it work in your favor. Remember a series of small commitments and positive affirmations will lead to the big decision taking care of itself.

Last but not least, try this homework assignment. Rephrase anything that you now say in statement form and turn it into a question. Remember, why tell when you can ask! My wife Jamie frequently talks in questions. It's crazy - she doesn't really "tell" me to do anything. She just asks questions. She'll say: "Babe, do you think this 500 pound piece of furniture will look better over here?" If I say yes, I'm moving it and if I say I'm not sure I'm still moving it! Either way, she always wins.

Knowing the secret of the yes momentum will help you as a buyer too. Whenever I'm in a situation where I find myself saying my second "yes," I start to think; "here it comes!" What's interesting is that you'll be able disconnect yourself from the situation because you know what's going on. No big deal if you really want what you're about to be persuaded to buy.

# Street Smart Secret # 13-
## Speak With Authority

People are silently begging to be led and guided.

The words you use are of extreme importance. But, of more importance is how you say the right words. We touched on this in my "Ultimate Success Formula."

It's what you say and how you say it that counts. You can say the same words in a week or UN-confident tone or you can speak with authority, conviction, passion and empathy. You can stand up straight or slouch over. You can look at everyone in the eyes and make a connection or you can look away and create a feeling of not caring.

Your authority can come from the credibility that you've already established. Your authority will also come from your tone and body language. It needs to be assertive and light a fire under those who you are attempting to persuade. NO. You don't have to be a 'pushy' person, but your authority must come through and show that you care.

Speak with good posture, always make eye contact and lead your prospect or your audience by the hand to convince them that you are the authority. Then, when you offer something that will make their lives better they will say YES!
When I train people that are new to the game, I find

that not speaking with authority is their biggest problem. I encourage them to study their products and services in more detail. I advise them to practice on their spouse or friends and do anything to get their pitch and tone to the point of being authoritative.

## How Lack of Authority Cost A Cable Company a Ton of Money!

When my wife and I moved from the great communist state of New Jersey to the "Live free or die" state of New Hampshire we had to make a few choices. One of them was: cable or satellite? We really don't watch much television. This was certainly going to be one of those decisions that came down to getting the best possible service for the price. We view television as a luxury not a necessity. High speed Internet, now that's a necessity!

I called the local cable company to find out about their different digital plans. I wanted to know what the basic package plus a couple of 'premium channels" would be. I was amazed by the total lack of "authority!" The sales rep seemed to have absolutely no clue about what I was asking. I basically controlled the whole conversation, which went something like this:

Me- Hi, I'm new to the area and we're moving into our new place in a couple of days. I wanted to find out what sort of digital cable, Internet and phone plans you have?
Clueless Cable Gal- Have you ever had service with us

before?

Time out! I know she was following a script. But even though you train your sales staff to follow a script does not mean they become robots! When I train sales people on scripts I am also very animate about what I call the human element. That's when I show them how to make the script sound 100% natural.

Me- No, I'm new to the area!

Clueless Cable Gal- Well what would you like to know?

Me- (Long pause, asking myself what language I'm speaking) Well, I want to know about digital cable, Internet and phone?

Clueless Cable Gal- Oh! (Sound of shuffling papers) Let me see, the basic digital package will be $129 per month, plus tax. If you want another box it's $6.95 per month, per box. Of course you'll need to pay an installation fee and your first month.

Me- Ok, what about premium channels like *HBO and Showtime*?

You can probably imagine the rest of the details so I won't cause you anymore pain. I then I called Direct TV. After I got through the easy-to-follow menu options, I was greeted by a sweet voice that said something to the effect of; "How may I help you get your service started today?"

I don't remember the details because the person was in control and speaking with authority the entire time. I felt at ease as she explained my option. She also informed me of the numerous special promotions I had coming to me as a first time customer. She came off with authority and led me by the hand so that I would make a decision and get going. And that's what I did!

Authority is more than being in charge. It's about communicating to the people you're influencing the fact that they are safe with you and that you know what you're doing. I don't remember the details of the conversation with the Direct TV rep because her authority and the way I was treated made me very relaxed and of course, easy to influence.

"Walk talk and act as though you were somebody, because you are! Let victory speak from your face and express itself in your manner."

# Street Smart Secret # 14- Always Give a "Reason Why" and Use the Word "Because"

Many, many years ago a famous advertising copywriter named John Kennedy wrote a book called *Reason Why Advertising.* He basically knew that one of the secrets that motivate people to buy is a strong reason. In the ground breaking book, *Influence: Science and Practice*, Robert Cialdini told of case studies where using just the word "because" helped increase compliance drastically.

Don't just have a sale or offer a discount. Give a method to your madness and you'll always be more believable. People have to believe you before they can be influenced by you.

You can put the word "because" in front of almost anything...

"Because you've been a customer for a month you get _____."

"Because my calendar fills up real quick, it's in your best interest to arrange a visit!"

Give a reason for a sale or discount...

"Because we had a flood and need to make room for the cleanup we are discounting the items that were saved."

"Because of this crazy weather we're discounting everything!"

Be as specific as possible! Dig deep for a powerful reason and you'll get great results.

# Street Smart Secret # 15- Limited Supplies, For Real!

We've heard it before, "Hurry supplies are limited, don't wait or you'll be locked out forever!"

There are a whole lot of variations to this message and principle, but the underlying truth is... Limited time and limited supplies work because we are all conditioned to want we can't have, want what is soon to be no longer available, and want what is in short supply.

We know this from the dating scene. The more you pursue, the more they run, the less you pursue the more they come to you. There are two ways to approach this very powerful persuasive principle:

## Attitude

Doesn't the person who is willing to walk away always get the better deal? Isn't the guy who is not all over the pretty girl begging for a shot usually the one she falls for? We had dinner guests one evening who were telling us about their daughter's dating life.

There was a wonderful gentleman who was "head over heels" for her. He was a successful attorney with a great house and financial stability. She dumped him because when he introduced her to his parents, they said, "So son, this is the mother of our grandchildren?" and he said, "Yes!" OUCH! This guy may be successful in his career, but I'm gathering he left his persuasive power and tactfulness in his desk drawer. He was certainly not attempting to limit his supply!

For salespeople and business owners, the worst perception you can give to your prospect is the perception of really needing the sale. The trick is to let the perception of being in short supply be something that takes care of itself.

If you work by appointment, stick to your times and respect the fact that your good prospects work this way as well. Example: If you 'call' on prospects you're better off sending a postcard or letter or at least check them out online before you go in. You're also better off going in with the idea to make arrangements for a planned meeting.

You can do this with your existing clients too. Why should anyone just be able to call you up or pop in on you whenever they please? Simply let people know that you work by appointment and they can send you an email to arrange a time to talk. If they prefer the phone allow them to leave you a message with a choice of some times for you to get back to them. I do quite a bit of phone consulting and each of my clients respects my time. They have no issues sending an email or calling to arrange a consultation.

I agree that answering the phone all the time is good customer service. But ask yourself: Is it you that should be answering or someone else? Can you get the phone answered constantly during business hours in a way that serves the caller and you? Are you prepared to develop a system?

You can let people know that if you are available you will get the phone. But, if getting an unexpected call will distract you from something else or you can't give the caller the attention they deserve then the caller should be ready to leave a message.

How can you make yourself more valuable and more persuasive if you are at everyone's beck and call? It is courteous to be available especially if this is how you get business. Just be sure to prioritize and work off a schedule. The easiest way to accomplish this is to be clear with your clients. My clients know that I will answer between certain hours if I am able to.

I always get a kick out of people who say they're available all the time. "Twenty-four hour emergency service" Or, "Call me with your real estate questions any time." No way can you be available all the time, offer good service and have a life! If you are in a business that would benefit from the whole "twenty-four hour service" thing great, do it, just be sure to fulfill. If you don't fulfill, you'll only upset your prospects and clients.

**Reality**

Think of how many clients and customers you want and need to achieve your life style, income, and business goals. Reverse engineer the process from the start. Meaning, even if you are just starting out put your attitude in place.

The real goal is to be in demand for 366 days out of the year! Once you are there (and even before you are there) you begin to be scarce in your supply causing others to want what they cannot have.

Basing this on reality will help you be truthful when using the 'limited supply' principle. This will really backfire on you if you are insincere about it.

Life is just too short to try to please everyone. When your best customers and clients get the message that you really are in short supply then they will want to hold on to you as long as you give them the quality, value and service they deserve.

Manage your business and run your life so you and your customers both benefit!

I a guy I was in Toastmasters with for a while, Harold Maxim, started his own accounting business at the age of sixty-two after he was laid off by a big company. Twelve years later, at age seventy-four, his client roster is full and he has more work than he can handle. He is not taking any more clients. He told me when he started he conveyed to his clients that one day he would be full, so if they liked his work, they should be sure to comply with his rules of doing business. Needless to say, Harold reverse-engineered the process.

# Street Smart Secret # 16- Entertain Them

Entertainment is the one of the highest grossing industries in the U.S. A CNBC report in 2006 revealed that the average American household spends about $2100 per year on different types of entertainment.

We spend money on sporting events, movies, television, vacations, amusement parks, and anything else that generates positive, relaxing, and fun emotions. The best and highest paid entertainers are the individuals and events that get you involved! They realize that people are moved and influenced by positive emotions, not just information.

As professional persuaders, it is our obligation to entertain and involve the people we are influencing. It is our job to generate positive results that lead to positive emotions for everyone. When you begin to understand and implement this concept into all of your presentations and every aspect of your business sales will come easier and with greater abundance.

A major form of influence is positive emotions, and a way to get positive emotion is through entertainment and involvement. If your audience, be it one person or one hundred, is just sitting there disengaged they will not be influenced by you.

We need the people listening to our presentations to

be on the edge of their seats. We need them laughing, smiling, and happy. We also need them focused when the time comes. We need them doing the same things that they would do when they go to the movies or attend a professional sporting event. Would they bring a newspaper to a football game or to a movie? No way, they don't want to miss a second of the action!

Make the shift from sales person/business owner, to entertainer and motivator. Let them come to you for the same reasons they spend the big bucks on everything else, to feel good and have fun!

With entertainment you get involvement and with involvement you get commitment and with commitment you have persuasive power. When you begin to entertain as well as educate you make everyone more relaxed and get their positive emotions going. When they view you as larger than life and envy your ability to captivate and inspire them, they will be influenced by you.

## It is not difficult

There was a gentleman named Ted in a BNI group I used to attend. BNI is a very effective networking organization. Anyway, each week the members of the group take one minute to say a little bit about their businesses. Ted always gets his message across in a way that makes the group laugh. And remember too it's not just about being funny, so don't worry if you are not "funny." It's about being memorable.

Like Shakespeare said, "Life is but a stage and we are all actors."

# Street Smart Secret # 17 Stack the Odds in Your Favor

Growing up in Philadelphia put me about fifty miles or so from Atlantic City. America's second favorite spot to roll the dice. Many of my teenaged buddies couldn't wait until the day that they would be able to go gamble. Not me!

Why, if I was so close all those years, can I only count the number of times on my one hand that I have actually went and put my dough on the table? I like the thrill of making money and I certainly love to be entertained. But what kept me away was the knowledge that the odds were against me. I'd much rather invest my time and money in activities and investments where I can stack the odds in my favor, wouldn't you? Let's talk about how we can put as many of the odds in our favor to help us persuade a group or individual to do what we want just about every single time.

## Pre-First Contact

Where the game of odds begins is before you come face to face with your prospect or audience. The odds start with your marketing and reputation. If it's good, you up your chances; if it's poor, you only hurt your chances. Make sure you're following good advice and marketing strategies that have a successful track record. You decrease your odds if you don't follow proven marketing, sales and persuasive principles.

The phone rings. Your manner, tone and persuasive skills will help you.

Use them to:

1) Build rapport by asking planed benefit oriented questions to control the conversation.

2) Spark curiosity by giving enough information, but not too much. You should give information that will cause the caller to want to 'see you in action.' You spark curiosity by painting a wonderful picture of the caller achieving all the benefits they want.

3) Get a solid appointment to see the individual/group or close the deal right on the phone.

Increase your odds by asking for all decision makers to be present during your meeting. Simply say; "Our first meeting is very special. Of course, I will be looking forward to meeting everyone that will have a say in this decision."

## Schedule for success

Arrange the meeting when you know you will be able to give this person or group your undivided attention. This goes with doing teleconferences too. You mess up your odds if you're on the phone with a potential client and you're also checking email. I believe doing so will actually kill brain cells too! In your personal life follow the same phone call etiquette. Think about how many fights you could avoid with your spouse if you would just give her your undivided attention. We're all guilty of this one.

## Initial contact

Stack the odds more in your favor simply by being a likable person so the prospect wants to do business with you. Do this by leaving nothing to chance. Make sure you're are clean, fresh and dressed for success. Greet the prospect graciously but not overwhelmingly. Be calm and cool. Then seat the prospect where you are in complete control of them and your environment. Remember you call the shots and you determine what happens next. If you are in the prospect's office and do not feel comfortable or in control politely say; "Can we sit here, you'll be better served if I'm more comfortable, I appreciate it" and then just move to where you want to sit.

## The Close

We'll assume that things are going well for you. Stack the odds in your favor by being sensitive to the fact that the prospect's stress level is naturally a tad higher. You must be the same great person or better when you ask them to invest in you, your products and services. Keep it simple and show a genuine interest! By the way, asking increases your odds dramatically. Be mindful of body language and vocal tone at this crucial moment of truth. Tie it all together and you're guaranteed to effectively influence and persuade most of the time.

# Street Smart Secret # 18- An Under Used Tool That Will Set You Apart

What is this under used tool that will set you apart?

It's one of those, as Dan Kennedy says: "little hinges that swing big doors." It's one of those little things that cause you to be remembered and the other guy forgotten. It's one of those things that you look for as a customer or client.

It takes a minute to put together so it doesn't have twenty moving parts or complicated instructions. One of its parts is very cheap and self-adhesive. It'll show up exactly where you want just about every single time, with rare exception.

It brings a glow to the eyes of folks and a smile to their faces. It lets them know that you are a consummate professional who they should take very seriously and appreciate. Why? Because this thing is so underused! What are we talking about here??

We're talking about the thank you note. Sorry, not totally earth shattering, so don't be disappointed! The 'thank you' note is used by people who are serious about success! The little extra effort it takes to write one and drop it in the mail is nothing compared to the return it brings! It gives you the "wow" factor. It makes people say "He really cares enough to take the time to write me a little note."

Regardless of what you do for a living, getting in the habit of writing thank you notes to your clients will go a long way in making you stand out in their minds as someone who is at the top of your game. You'll actually stand out because most folks are not expecting to receive one. The thank you note simply confirms that your clients are dealing with a professional!

So get in the habit of sending a few notes per week, and you'll see a big return on the little time and postage that you invest.

# Street Smart Secret # 19: Social Media Marketing is Really Online Networking

By Chuck Sink

Engaging customers and potential customers in social media is very tricky and generally requires giving something. Let's keep this concept blunt and simple. Nobody cares about your company or the success of your business. They have neither obligation nor desire to share your company message and be your loyal brand steward unless they will benefit from doing so. Before posting, sharing content or promoting your page, always ask yourself: What's in it for them?

People are on Social Media mostly for 4 reasons - the **4 E's** of social media engagement: **E**go, **E**ntertainment, **E**ducation and **E**nrichment. Companies have to feed those desires and needs or they will be ignored in this space. When interacting with Likes (Friends), Connections, Followers, Circles, Fans, etc. you're really networking with them online and you need to bring something to the table or you'll be thought of as just another self promoter or corporate advertiser.

Social media is about online networking more than anything else. The same principles apply as when meeting people face to face. You need to share ideas, develop relationships and nurture friendships. The best B2C brands on Facebook interact with consumers in a way that feels one-on-one to them. Coke, Starbucks, Oreo, Redbull, Converse, Skittles and Playstation are among the most Liked brands on Facebook. Check out their pages and see for yourself how well they engage consumers.

LinkedIn is a great business forum to share ideas, best practices and connect with likeminded businesspeople. Twitter is a world of real time discussion in countless categories and a wellspring of ideas and fresh information. It's an amazing real-time search engine of online conversations surrounding extremely narrow or broad topics. Facebook is a great connector of people to share one-on-one or group dialog. Its potential reach is enormous! An entire chapter would only scratch the surface of Facebook's viral – network marketing potential.

Google+, YouTube, Foursquare, StumbleUpon, Digg, Reddit, blogs... There are so many platforms today. They all keep us linked and grow our networks, leading ultimately to profitable relationships so long as we stick with the 4 As and 4 Ps of social media; that is to be:

Active – Participate.
Attractive – Position value.
Alert – Pay attention.
Accessible – Permit dialog.

So let's be social when attempting to grow our businesses using social media. Your friends and followers are just like you and me. Remember those 4

Es. We all have Egos and love to be recognized. Everyone enjoys Entertainment. Our inquisitive minds seek Education. For ourselves and our families we want Enrichment. How will your business feed those desires online using the myriad social media platforms freely available to you?

*Chuck Sink is a marketing consultant and owner of Chuck Sink Link, specializing in copywriting and online content strategies. Email: chuck@chucksink.com  Web: www.chucksink.com*

# Street Smart Secret # 20 Don't Subscribe To the Myths About Selling and Persuasion

Selling and Persuasion are skills that are filled with misconceptions. Often these misconceptions keep even the most eager individual from fulfilling their destiny. You may believe a few myths about selling that prevent you from achieving your full potential. Read on to find out five common myths about selling. Find out how you can avoid these pitfalls and be on your way to mastering the valuable skill of selling and persuasion!

What are common myths?

**Selling Myth #1:** Sales people are all liars, cheats, and thieves.
There may be a portion of sales people that fit this nasty reputation, but this occurs in other professions such as lawyers, doctors, and bankers too. Being a liar, cheater, or thief is a personal shortcoming. It has nothing to do with the sales profession. This is a distinction that needs to be understood and conveyed.

Selling, when practiced honestly and in a professional manner, is the highest calling. A great salesman once said, "Sell the sizzle, not the steak." He also said "Nothing happens until somebody sells something." This means that you can have the greatest invention in the history of the world, but if you don't try to sell it then it will rust in your garage. And sales people are the people that will prevent your invention from gathering rust in your garage.

Sales people are the people that make the world work. They provide a tremendous service by bringing new ideas, solutions, and much more to people.

**Selling Myth #2:** Sales seminars and advice are too expensive.
If you find a well-respected sales seminar then the cost is well worth it. Many people claim that they want to know the secrets of the sales gurus, yet when it comes time to invest in learning these secrets, they become scared.

People don't realize that many sales seminars that cost hundreds or a few thousand dollars are worth every penny. They shy away from these because they aren't as much of an accepted form of learning as traditional education. For example, they are willing to pay $40,000, $50,000, even $60,000 a year to earn their MBA in a traditional learning environment. Yet, they won't spend far less on a sales seminar. A good consultant can also help you shortcut the time it takes you to become successful by speeding up your learning curve.

**Selling Myth #3:** Learning to be a top sales person is too difficult and the resources are out of the reach of the public.
This couldn't be farther from the truth. Selling is the highest calling in the American free enterprise system.

This free enterprise system has extended its reach to the global economy. The information you need to be good at selling is readily available.

**Selling Myth #4:** You should know every sales tactic and strategy of every sales guru in order to be successful.
Trying to learn every technique from every guru is not only confusing, but very tiring. Instead, you should choose a philosophy of one person or a select few. Then study everything this person has said, written, and done.

A word of caution: Don't bounce from resource to resource thinking that the secret answer will be in the next book, CD, or DVD. You have to realize that the answer is within yourself.

**Selling Myth #5:** Selling is too complicated.
Too many sales people and sale trainers over-complicate the selling process. They may do this to justify their existence. The reality is that selling should be a straightforward process. It can be broken down to a ten-step presentation about a quality product that is competitively priced. You should have a scripted presentation ready to go.

Did you believe any of these myths in the past? If so, throw your old misconceptions out the door. Right now!

# Street Smart Secret # 21- Ask, But Please, Ask In The Right Way

I was at seminar listening to Jack Canfield. Jack Canfield and Mark Victor Hansen are the geniuses behind the publishing phenomenon; *Chicken Soup for The Soul.* Anyway, he said something that is worth repeating. He said, "Just ask because before you asked the answer was no, so even if the person says no you are still in the same position. But, if they say yes you are now better off. Really what do you have to lose?"

I think the strategy of asking is a sure way of stepping on the accelerator of your life. But when you think about it the way Jack puts it, the fear of asking just melts away and you're off to the races.

In your life, think of the times when asking made a difference for you. Could you imagine what would have happened if you didn't ask? If you are married or in a great relationship right now, how would things be if you hadn't asked your mate for the chance to get to know her?

I really believe that where you are right now has a great deal to do with the things you have asked for and the things you have not asked for. The fact of the matter is that in persuasion the "askers" make it happen. But be careful how you ask!
**You can begin asking for simple things, the right way, in**

**your everyday life.** Let me give you some examples:

When we moved from New Jersey to New Hampshire we brought our outdoor grill with us. The only problem was that the grill we owned was a natural gas grill and long story short, we had no way to use it. So we gave that grill to my parents and then went to Home Depot for a new propane powered grill.

As we were getting ready to check out, via the customer service desk, I said in a soft and friendly tone; "Did I read something about free delivery?" The clerk said in a nice tone back; "I don't believe we are doing free delivery, it costs $60 for up to sixty miles." I said; "Oh, we only live about five miles away, but is there a way we can get free delivery?" Then she said: "I don't know." "I said, Could you ask your manager for us?" "Sure" was her response. What happened next was interesting. They didn't go for the free delivery. But they gave us use of their flatbed rental (no charge) so we could easily get the grill home. If I didn't ask we would have either paid $60 for delivery or, we would have had to comeback at another time to get the grill after removing the kids' car seats and then figuring out who was going to watch the girls while we went back to pick up the grill.

When I check into a hotel I always ask for a special rate. I have saved as much as twenty percent on some occasions. The next thing I'll do upon checking in is to ask; "So what's for breakfast, do you have any coupons I could use?" It is rare that I am turned down for a free breakfast coupon. I'm talking hot breakfast not continental either!

It's amazing how many sales people don't simply ask for the order. The best way to do so is with an alternate of choice or an "A or B" option question. When I sold memberships I'd always offer the monthly option or the cash savings/paid in full option. Prospects would simply choose the one that fit their budgets best.

End your emails and print correspondence with clear, firm and polite directions that ask the reader to take the action you desire. It is extremely important in print to be extremely concise and leave nothing to chance, NO assumptions!

I like to pad my requests with phrases like:
"Would you mind..?"
"Does it make sense to...?"
"Is it ok if...?"
"Would it be OK to...?"

Phrases like the ones above soften the asking process and help you fly under the radar.

And don't be afraid to ask for help and advice from those who you think are in a position to help you.

There's really no need to assume the answer will be no. The truth is you never know until you ask! Asking will improve your business and personal life! Feel Free to ask "Mike D!" Go to www.AskMikeD.com

# Chapter 22 - Base Everything on The Truth!

The TRUTH!

Personal Magnetism is a mixture of rugged Honesty, Pulsating Energy, and Self-Organized Intelligence. The TRUTH (spelled with a big T) is the strongest weapon we can use, whether we're fighting for a cause, marketing ourselves, or making a group or one to one sale. TRUTH unconsciously makes you strong, aggressive and super persuasive!

A lie is the weapon of a weak individual. The person that uses truth will, without realizing it, appear frank and sincere. Nothing creates confidence more easily than frankness and sincerity!

There is no come back to the TRUTH, no alibi, no hereafters, and no explanations are required. It is a vital force as though you could take it out, hold it, look at it and feel it.

Every Master of Persuasion uses the TRUTH!

# Chapter 23 - Sales and Marketing Lessons From La Cosa Nostra

When you grow in South Philadelphia with an Italian American background you can't help but develop a sort of interest and fascination with La Cosa Nostra (another word for Mafia).

When I was twelve, back in 1992, I watched as a brutal war between two mafia 'families' played out. Bullets spayed just two blocks from my middle school in an attempt to 'whack' Joseph 'Skinny Joey" Merlino and his closest confidant. Merlino lived and ended up taking over as head of the Philadelphia mob after John Stanfa ended up in jail for Racketeering and Murder charges. Those were some crazy days. Merlino's reign actually went on for a while until he got "pinched" in 2001.

I am firm believer that there are lessons to be gleaned from every experience, whether you are participant or a spectator. I'm glad to say that I was a spectator to the above mentioned events and not a participant! While others were enamored by the *500 SL's* and the appearances of financial success that the mafia portrayed, I knew that the laws of the universe and of the United States would ultimately prevail.

Many of my teenage 'friends' were fascinated with the Philly mob for the wrong reasons. I was only impressed by the way their organization ran like a business.

As you can see, it was easy for us South Philly guys to become a little interested in the mafia. Hey, it's no different than a guy or girl who is interested in history or something like that. The sales and marketing lesson is coming....

My interest led me to learning about Frank Costello. Costello was one of the real life characters that the *God Father* movies were based on. Costello ultimately craved respect in the "legit" business world and often served to bridge the gap between the real world and the underworld. Now the sales marketing lesson...

Costello accumulated his wealth and power as a bootlegger after the Volstead Act became law in 1920 and led to the prohibition of alcohol. From the beginning Costello never let bootlegging be his only source of revenue. He had many 'rackets' going (both 'legit and not) to hedge against the day that alcohol would become legal again and put him out of the bootlegging business. That day came in 1933. He was extremely wealthy already and had so many productive sources of business that it didn't matter to him that he could no longer be a bootlegger.

Some simple lessons...

What has worked in the past CANNOT be expected to work forever. It must be improved on as the statistics of your business reveal the current trends.

One source of new business is dangerous if that source stops working or is no longer available.

Multiple streams of revenue from different sources will never hurt your business. It will help you hedge against any one source drying up.

Diversify your business, marketing, selling and persuasion efforts or else Bruno may come knocking.

OK, it's been fun, I hope you enjoyed our time together. Be sure you check out the next couple pages because I'd love to serve you in the future.

*"Never let 'em catch you acting. The art is HIDING the art."*

Michael Caine

# Resources Available To You From The Author

## Bring Mike D. in to Speak for Your Group!

Mike D. can speak for your club, company or organization. Whether you are looking for a keynote presentation, a breakout session or a workshop, Mike can be the ideal speaker for your next event or meeting. Mike is not a "Motivational Speaker" - he is the world's only "Mobilizational Speaker," because he moves his audience members to action! Below is a partial list of his presentations. For updated info visit: www.AskMikeD.com/services/speaking

## "The Success Secret That Never Fails" / "Motion Before Motivation"

In this keynote or breakout session, Mike will cover the key points that your audience needs to get in motion and make things happen quickly. This talk will inspire them to get into action so they can reach team and personal goals.

## "Magic Words That Bring You Clients and Customers"

This talk is ideal for marketers, salespeople, business owners and anyone whose results are tied to the cooperation of others. Mike will cover Persuasion Secrets of the written and spoken word so your audience can immediately go out and start selling more effectively.

## "Put Your Business in The Palm of Their Hands: The Secrets of Mobile Marketing."

This is one of Mike's most requested talks. He'll give your audience a firm understanding of Mobile Marketing. He'll deliver the information in a fun way and show them how to implement what they learn.

## "7 Ways to Get Your Business and Personal Life Moving"

The title of this talk pretty much sums it up!

For queries and questions regarding availability, please send an email to Mike@AskMikeD.com or call 267.992.2970

## Website Design, Copywriting, Online and Offline Marketing Consulting and Business Strategy

If you are looking for fresh ideas and insights to propel your business forward, then this program may be for you. Mike will help you design and implement marketing campaigns and strategies. Mike will help you turn the features of your business into irresistible benefits that your ideal customers will be attracted to. Mike will help you uncover the buried treasure in your current business and open up new opportunities and income streams that you've been overlooking. Mike's team can design a website for you that is found by your best prospects and quickly turns them into clients.

Visit: CyberspaceToYourPlace.com

# About the Author

Mike Dolpies (AKA Mike D.) is a Veteran Small Business Owner, Consultant and Speaker. He started his first business just six months out of high school at the age of eighteen. He speaks for corporations and associations on the topics of Success, Peak Performance, Publicity, Mobile Marketing and Ethical Persuasion. Mike's practical and entertaining advice is based on his years of real world experience and his constant and never-ending learning. He can be reached at www.cyberspacetoyourplace.com or www.askmiked.com

Like Quotes?

Get some of Mike D's Original Quotes At...
http://www.askmiked.com/about-us/quotes-by-mike-d/

www.ingramcontent.com/pod-product-compliance
Lightning Source LLC
Chambersburg PA
CBHW060610200326
41521CB00007B/722